SPELLIN

for 2ND GRADE

2,000 WORDS
Every Kid Should Know

Grade 2 English
Ages 7-8

ABOUT THIS BOOK

Using a **fresh approach** to spellings lists, this illustrated collection of Spelling Words is designed **to make spelling fun** for children whilst helping them master essential spelling rules by the end of Grade 2.

Containing **2,000** carefully selected **level-appropriate** words, this book is made up of **70** Themed Spellings Lists that

- Have **brightly-colored illustrated backgrounds** and **engaging titles**
- Cover **loads of topics** that **actually interest children** such as wild animals, magic shows, and the beach
- Relate to other **areas covered at school** including continents & landforms, the human body, and the four seasons
- Target **key words that children overuse** (e.g. 'give', 'eat', and 'go')
- Quietly introduce **specific areas of spelling** that children need to know (e.g. silent letters, prefixes, doubling consonants, plural nouns, and homophones)
- Are made up of **25 to 30 words each**

HOW TO USE IT

All the **lists are self-contained**, so you can work through them **in order**, or, you can dip in to use them for **focused practice**. And, as these lists are themed, they are **also a useful resource** for a range of **writing projects and exercises**.

For your convenience, an **Index** to the **spelling rules, patterns, and themed areas** dealt with by each of the lists is included at the **back of the book** on page 40.

Published by STP Books
An imprint of Swot Tots Publishing Ltd
124 City Road
London EC1V 2NX

www.swottotspublishing.com

Text, design, illustrations and layout © Swot Tots Publishing Ltd
First published 2024

Swot Tots Publishing Ltd have asserted their moral right under the Copyright, Designs and Patents Act, 1988, to be identified as the author of this work.

Typeset, cover design, and inside concept design by Swot Tots Publishing Ltd.

British Library Cataloguing-in-Publication Data. A catalogue record for this book is available from the British Library.

ISBN 978-1-912956-47-0

CONTENTS

CONTENTS Cont.

Double Trouble

kid	drum	drop
kidding	drumming	dropping
skid	trim	stop
skidding	trimming	stopping
dig	grin	star
digging	grinning	starring
hug	run	hit
hugging	running	hitting
wag	win	sit
wagging	winning	sitting

Spooky Spell-ing!

bone	alarming	cackle
broomstick	bizarre	curse
cauldron	bloodcurdling	enchant
cemetery	chilling	haunt
cobweb	demonic	hex
eyeball	fearful	imprison
gravestone	grisly	moan
lantern	gruesome	panic
poison	spectral	spook
skull	unsettling	terrify

Chomp, Chomp, Chomp

attack	gulp	snack
binge	lick	stuff
chew	munch	swallow
chomp	nibble	tuck in
cram	nosh	wolf
crunch	peck	
devour	polish off	
gobble	scarf	
gorge	scoff	
graze	scrunch	

Ow? Uh? Or? Oor? Oh My!

our	four	tourist
hour	pour	courier
flour	mourn	contour
sour	court	detour
scour	course	gourmet
courage	source	
journal	fourth	
journey	fourteen	
flourish	courtside	
nourish	courtroom	

Repeat After Re-

reappear	refill	reshuffle
rearrange	reheat	resurface
rebuild	reintegrate	retake
recalculate	reintroduce	rethink
reconsider	relocate	retrace
recreate	renew	retry
recycle	reorganize	reuse
redefine	repay	review
rediscover	replay	revisit
redistribute	reread	rewrite

Reds, Blues, Greens...

blue	fuchsia	coral
aquamarine	shell pink	crimson
cyan	purple	maroon
navy blue	indigo	salmon
turquoise	lavender	yellow
green	magenta	canary yellow
lime	mauve	straw
olive	plum	hue
teal	violet	shade
pink	red	tint

Silent, But Deadly I

catacomb	doubt	plumber
catacombs	doubtful	plumbing
climb	honeycomb	subtle
climbing	jamb	succumb
comb	lamb	succumbed
combed	limb	succumbing
crumb	limbs	thumb
crumbs	numb	thumbed
debt	numbed	tomb
debts	numbing	tombs

Happy Endings I

adventurous	humorous	perilous
ambiguous	infamous	poisonous
cavernous	jealous	pompous
dangerous	joyous	ravenous
enormous	ludicrous	ridiculous
famous	mountainous	rigorous
generous	nervous	tremendous
glamorous	numerous	venomous
grievous	odorous	vigorous
humongous	ominous	virtuous

Get Creative I

aggressive	dignified	muddied
alert	famished	outlandish
astounding	frail	plodding
beady	glittering	pretentious
bewildered	hair-raising	realistic
candid	inquisitive	shimmery
charming	jittery	sluggish
combative	luscious	traumatic
crotchety	magnetic	triumphant
dainty	major	unwieldy

Ch- Ch- Chaos!

ache	chemical	monarch
anchor	chemistry	ocher
arachnid	choir	orchestra
architect	cholera	orchid
bronchitis	chord	pachyderm
chameleon	chorus	scheme
chaos	echo	scholar
chaotic	mechanic	stomach
character	melancholy	technical
chasm	mocha	technology

On The Hunt!

alligator	jaguar	raccoon
bald eagle	killer whale	rattlesnake
buzzard	Komodo dragon	snow leopard
cougar	lion	tiger
crocodile	mongoose	whale shark
dingo	moray eel	
electric eel	osprey	
falcon	otter	
grizzly bear	polar bear	
hawk	python	

Is It 'EL'...

angel	hotel	parcel
bagel	hovel	pixel
cancel	jewel	rebel
caramel	kestrel	shrivel
compel	label	snivel
cudgel	level	travel
diesel	marvel	trowel
easel	mongrel	tunnel
fuel	novel	vowel
gravel	panel	weasel

...Or 'LE'?

able	needle	cuddle
buckle	people	giggle
candle	sample	kettle
cradle	stable	muddle
crumple	startle	puddle
girdle	tumble	puzzle
grumble	battle	riddle
humble	bottle	rubble
mingle	bubble	shuttle
mumble	cattle	skittle

CRASH! BANG! WALLOP!

bang	peal	piercing
bellow	roar	ringing
blare	slam	screaming
blast	thud	screeching
boom	thump	shouting
chime	bawling	shrieking
clang	deafening	squawking
clatter	earsplitting	thundering
crash	hollering	yelling
honk	howling	yowling

100S! 1000S! 10S OF 1000S!

hundred	quadrillion	mega-
hundredth	quadrillionth	giga-
thousand	quintillion	tera-
thousandth	quintillionth	infinity
million	decillion	bazillion
millionth	centillion	bazillionth
billion	googol	gazillion
billionth	googolplex	gazillionth
trillion	hect-	zillion
trillionth	kilo-	zillionth

Un- The Undone

unarmed	uneasy	unstable
unavoidable	unexpected	unstoppable
unaware	unfair	unsuitable
unbeaten	unfed	untamed
unboxed	unharmed	unthinkable
uncanny	unimpressed	untied
uncaring	unjustly	untimely
uncommon	unnecessary	unwanted
undone	unresolved	unwrapped
unearthed	unsolved	unzipped

M—y—sterious Y

calypso	mystical	sympathize
crypt	mystified	symphonic
crystal	myth	symptom
cygnet	oxygen	system
gym	physical	typical
hymn	pyramid	
lynx	rhythm	
lyric	rhythmic	
lyrical	syllable	
mysterious	syllabus	

As Fresh As A Daisy

anemone	daisy	lotus
bluebell	dandelion	marigold
buttercup	foxglove	pansy
camellia	geranium	poppy
carnation	honeysuckle	primrose
cornflower	hyacinth	rose
cowslip	iris	snowdrop
crocus	jasmine	sunflower
daffodil	lilac	tulip
dahlia	lily	wallflower

Bestow & Beyond

award	donate	hand over
bequeath	endow	impart
bestow	entrust	invest
cater	equip	lavish
confer	furnish	offer
contribute	gift	parcel out
deliver	give away	pass on
dispense	grant	present
distribute	hand down	provide
dole out	hand out	reward

That Doesn't Look Right I

twelfth	guard	different
thirty	guest	heard
forty	build	heart
ninety	quite	learn
achieve	appear	money
believe	busy	alright
friend	calm	always
lied	government	until
thief	calendar	question
view	definitely	answer

Happy Endings II

anxiously	sadly	largely
cautiously	seriously	rarely
chiefly	slowly	savagely
correctly	suddenly	wisely
instantly	violently	accidentally
lightly	absolutely	generally
loudly	bravely	mentally
quickly	fiercely	morally
quietly	genuinely	carefully
roughly	immediately	playfully

On The Map

Africa	Pacific Ocean	island
Antarctica	ocean	landmass
Asia	sea	desert
Australia	gulf	delta
Europe	river	valley
North America	lake	canyon
South America	waterfall	mountain
Arctic Ocean	continent	grid
Atlantic Ocean	peninsula	legend
Indian Ocean	archipelago	scale

Ooh... Shiny!

aluminum	foil	silver
brass	glitter	sparklers
Christmas ornaments	gold	stainless steel
coins	lipstick	tinsel
copper	metallic paint	trumpet
crystals	metallic thread	
diamonds	nail polish	
disco ball	patent leather	
eye shadow	platinum	
fireworks	sequins	

Hey! Eight Reindeer!

rein	freight	convey
reindeer	neigh	disobey
unveil	neighbor	drey
veil	overweight	hey
vein	reign	obey
beige	sleigh	prey
eight	weigh	survey
eighteen	weighed	they
eighth	weight	whey
eighty	weightless	whey-faced

What's A Person Who...

barber	forester	publisher
bookseller	hairdresser	singer
broadcaster	hunter	smuggler
climber	interpreter	songwriter
cobbler	interviewer	steelworker
dancer	jailer	storyteller
employer	leader	trainer
explorer	painter	trickster
firefighter	printer	writer
footballer	programmer	zookeeper

Rattling On

babble	gibber	tittle-tattle
blab	gossip	twitter
blabber	jabber	waffle
blather	natter	yak
blither	patter	yammer
burble	prattle	
chat	rattle off	
chatter	rattle on	
gab	run on	
gabble	tattle	

Look At Dis-

disagree
disallow
disappoint
disarm
disband
disbar
disbelief
disconnect
discount
discourage

discredit
disembark
dishonest
dishonor
disinfect
disinformation
dislike
dislocate
disloyal
dismiss

dismount
disorder
disown
displace
displease
disprove
disregard
disrepair
dissatisfy
distrust

Super Sweet!

amaretto
Baked Alaska
banana split
biscotti
brownies
chocolate chip cookie
cutout cookie
doughnuts
drop cookie
fortune cookie

fudge
gingerbread
gingersnap
jelly roll
ladyfingers
lane cake
macaron
meringue
peach cobbler
petit four

s'more
snickerdoodle
sundae
truffle
upside-down cake

Splendid Spring

March	piglets	sunny
April	tadpoles	sunshine
May	bloom	windy
bunnies	blossom	buzzing
butterflies	bud	cheerful
chicks	bulbs	chirping
ducklings	breeze	fresh
fledglings	brisk	singing
foals	outdoors	sprouting
lambs	showers	tweeting

Sumptuous Summer

June	sun hat	stifling
July	suntan	flip-flops
August	tan	sandals
ants	blazing	shorts
bees	boiling	swimsuit
flies	cloudless	summer camp
wasps	hazy	museum
seagulls	humid	amusement park
sunbathe	muggy	swimming pool
sunburned	scorching	playground

Fabulous Fall

September	berries	earthy
October	conkers	nippy
November	falling leaves	rainy
gather	pine cones	soggy
harvest	orchard	stormy
hibernate	pumpkin	amber
migrate	blustery	burgundy
reap	chilly	golden
wilt	crisp	russet
acorns	damp	rust brown

Wondrous Winter

December	snowy	cough
January	treacherous	shiver
February	wintry	sneeze
arctic	boots	sniffle
biting	fleece	snuffle
freezing	duffle coat	ice skates
frosty	mittens	skis
frozen	scarves	snowboards
icy	sweater	snowballs
slushy	parka	snowman

Joining Forces

anteater	fishpond	newspaper
ballroom	footpath	nightfall
bedroom	hardback	nobody
blackbird	homework	pinstripe
bluebird	horseshoe	saucepan
candlestick	indoors	scarecrow
carsick	inkpot	signpost
daybreak	jigsaw	weekend
earthworm	limelight	whiteboard
firecracker	moonbeam	windmill

IT'S MAGIC!

magician	bending	nimbleness
assistant	conjuring	sleight of hand
birdcage	disappearing	teleportation
doves	hiding	tricks
handkerchief	tapping	vanish into thin air
magic wand	entertainment	
playing cards	grand finale	
rope	hocus-pocus	
silk scarves	illusion	
top hat	invisible	

Enough Said

announced	complained	cried
declared	groaned	sobbed
pronounced	grumbled	wailed
stated	moaned	wept
uttered	whined	whimpered
roared	breathed	asked
screamed	mumbled	inquired
shouted	muttered	interrogated
thundered	sighed	questioned
yelled	whispered	quizzed

Get Creative II

accentuate	disdain	infuriate
accomplish	embellish	initiate
bombard	enrich	intensify
champion	exhilarate	magnify
cherish	foresee	ransom
combat	gladden	shatter
deduce	hatch	squander
depict	hinder	transgress
detest	illuminate	triumph
devote	indulge	vanquish

Are You Sure...Or Ture?

leisure	departure	picture
measure	feature	rapture
pleasure	fracture	sculpture
pressure	furniture	signature
treasure	future	stature
adventure	gesture	structure
capture	lecture	temperature
caricature	literature	texture
creature	nature	torture
culture	overture	vulture

Determiner-ation!

a	many	that
an	more	these
the	most	those
each	much	my
every	few	your
both	fewer	his
all	fewest	her
any	little	its
several	less	our
some	this	their

Have You Ever Been To...

Albuquerque	Honolulu	Nashville
Atlanta	Huntsville	New Orleans
Baltimore	Indianapolis	New York City
Boston	Kansas City	Oklahoma City
Charlotte	Las Vegas	Omaha
Chicago	Los Angeles	Philadelphia
Columbus	Louisville	Phoenix
Colorado Springs	Miami	Portland
Dallas	Milwaukee	Seattle
Detroit	Minneapolis	Virginia Beach

Silent, But Deadly II

knack	knickknack	know
knapsack	knife	knowledge
knave	knight	known
knaves	knit	knows
knead	knitted	knuckle
knee	knives	
kneel	knob	
knell	knock	
knelt	knoll	
knew	knot	

Fruit Cups

apricot	date	papaya
avocado	fig	passion fruit
banana	gooseberry	peach
black currant	grapefruit	pineapple
blackberry	kiwi	pomegranate
blueberry	lemon	raspberry
cantaloupe	mandarin	red currant
cherry	mango	satsuma
clementine	melon	strawberry
cranberry	nectarine	tangerine

Lots 'N Lots 'N Lots

girls	leaves	children
boys	lives	women
pencils	thieves	men
radishes	wives	businesswomen
gases	heroes	businessmen
torches	potatoes	mice
babies	tomatoes	oxen
fairies	pianos	teeth
families	photos	bacteria
spies	cellos	sarcophagi

EYES ON THE BALL!

American football
badminton
baseball
basketball
billiards
bowling
croquet
football
golf
handball

hockey
lacrosse
miniature golf
netball
paintball
polo
rounders
rugby
snooker
soccer

squash
table tennis
tennis
volleyball
water polo

Departure Time

abandon
clear out
cut out
decamp
depart
desert
emigrate
escape
evacuate
exit

flee
fly
forsake
immigrate
leave
make off
pull stakes
quit
retire
retreat

run away
set out
take off
vacate
withdraw

HAPPY ENDINGS III

electrician	excursion	version
mathematician	expansion	action
musician	explosion	creation
comprehension	extension	donation
conclusion	inclusion	edition
confusion	invasion	election
conversion	occasion	equation
decision	revision	invention
division	supervision	option
exclusion	television	reaction

Wish You Were Here!

expedition	bed-and-breakfast	luggage
spring break	campsite	passport
trip	lodge	photographs
vacation	airplane	postcard
voyage	ferry	suitcase
camping	motor home	ticket
cruise	train	explore
hiking	backpack	unpack
safari	baggage	visit
sightseeing	guidebook	wander

Theseus & Co.

Achilles	Andromeda	centaur
Ajax	Arachne	Chimera
Bellerophon	Ariadne	Cyclops
Hector	Atalanta	gorgon
Heracles	Cassandra	Harpies
Jason	Electra	Hydra
Odysseus	Hecuba	Minotaur
Oedipus	Helen of Troy	Pegasus
Perseus	Pandora	Satyr
Theseus	Penelope	Sphinx

To-ing & Fro-ing

inside out	now and then	end to end
right side up	out and about	from head to toe
upside down	in circles	from start to finish
back and forth	through and through	from top to bottom
give-and-take	to and fro	from top to toe
here and now	up and about	
here and there	up and down	
hither and thither	yes and no	
in and out	back to front	
left and right	back-to-back	

EW!!

clammy	grungy	slimy
cruddy	gummy	slippery
dingy	gunky	slithery
funky	icky	sludgy
fusty	mucky	smelly
gloppy	muddy	stenchy
gooey	musty	sticky
greasy	oozy	stinky
grimy	reeky	sweaty
grubby	scuzzy	yucky

These Are Bugging Me...

bedbug	honeybee	stick insect
beetle	hornet	termite
bumblebee	ladybug	wasp
chafer	locust	water scorpion
dragonfly	louse	weevil
earwig	mayfly	
firefly	midge	
flea	mosquito	
fruit fly	moth	
grasshopper	silverfish	

Ssss...

adolescent
ascend
ascendant
ascent
crescent
descend
descent
disciple
disciplinary
discipline

fascinate
fascination
isosceles
muscles
scene
scenery
scenic
scent
scented
science

scientific
scientist
scimitar
scissors
scythe

NUT & SEED MIX

almonds
Brazil nuts
breadnuts
cashew nuts
chestnuts
hazelnuts
hickories
kola nuts
macadamia nuts
pecans

pine nuts
pistachios
walnuts
aniseed
cardamom seeds
chia seeds
coriander seeds
flaxseed
hempseed
linseed

mustard seeds
poppy seeds
pumpkin seeds
sesame seeds
sunflower seeds

That Doesn't Look Right II

Tuesday	percent	difficult
Wednesday	circle	break
Thursday	excel	breath
juice	recent	breathe
guide	regular	earth
guile	separate	group
guilt	surprise	library
quiet	possible	lollipop
quarter	probable	minute
addition	awful	threw

Gray Scale

alabaster	iron gray	raven
ash	ivory	sable
battleship gray	jet	slate gray
charcoal gray	mineral gray	snow
cream	nickel	steel gray
dove gray	off-white	
ebony	oyster white	
eggshell	pearl	
gray	pewter	
gunmetal	pitch-black	

All Over The Place!

above	start	about
below	finish	across
over	on	by
under	off	from
inside	in front	onto
outside	behind	
before	with	
after	between	
front	almost	
back	near	

"Might" Sounds Like...

appetite	spite	outright
bite	unite	plight
despite	website	upright
excite	white	light
ignite	write	daylight
invite	bright	floodlight
kite	delight	moonlight
mite	eyesight	twilight
polite	flight	midnight
recite	fright	tonight

Whodunit?!

camouflaged	unknown	notified
concealed	cracked	owned up
disguised	explained	witnessed
hidden	revealed	betrayed
secretive	solved	double-crossed
veiled	uncovered	
baffling	unmasked	
mystifying	confessed	
puzzling	informed	
unclear	leaked	

HAPPY ENDINGS IV

adaptation	fixation	presentation
affirmation	formation	reformation
alteration	foundation	relaxation
confirmation	importation	resignation
consideration	information	segmentation
consultation	invalidation	taxation
deportation	limitation	temptation
expectation	liquidation	transformation
exploitation	misinformation	vexation
exultation	plantation	visitation

Sip 'N Slurp

almond milk	grape juice	mocktail
cocoa	green tea	orange juice
coconut milk	hot chocolate	orangeade
coconut water	ice-cream soda	rooibos tea
coffee	kombucha	root beer
cola	lassi	sherbet
cream soda	lemonade	smoothie
energy drink	matcha	soda water
ginger ale	milkshake	soybean milk
ginger beer	mineral water	tonic water

Kitchen Kit

air fryer	chopsticks	mold
baking sheet	colander	pepper mill
blender	food processor	potato masher
bottle opener	French press	rolling pin
bread knife	griddle	sieve
can opener	grill	spatula
carving knife	juicer	toaster oven
casserole	ladle	vegetable peeler
cheese cutter	measuring cup	whisk
chopping block	microwave oven	wok

Jack Be Quick...

bolt	hurtle	skip
bounce	jump	skyrocket
bound	leap	speed
charge	leapfrog	spring
chase	lollop	sprint
dart	pounce	stampede
dash	race	streak
gallop	rush	trip
hop	scramble	vault
hurdle	shoot	zoom

Slowly AND Surely?

amble	lag	putter
clump	limp	ramble
dally	linger	shamble
dawdle	loaf	shuffle
dodder	loiter	slog
drag	loll	stagger
drift	lounge	stroll
hang around	lumber	stumble
hobble	lurch	totter
idle	plod	trudge

Head-Scratchers

ball	heal	road
bawl	heel	rode
bare	meat	sew
bear	meet	sow
chews	pain	tail
choose	pane	tale
cymbal	pair	throne
symbol	pear	thrown
groan	poor	tide
grown	pore	tied

Robin Hood & Co.

Robin Hood	King Richard	outlaw
Maid Marian	Locksley	forest laws
Merry Men	Sherwood Forest	peasants
Little John	Crusades	exploits
Friar Tuck	Lincoln green	generosity
Will Scarlet	hero	oppression
Alan-a-Dale	archer	thievery
Sheriff of Nottingham	swordsman	ballads
Guy of Gisborne	nobleman	fame
Prince John	yeoman	folktales

Body Language

ankle	hip	ribs
armpit	intestine	shin
arteries	joints	shoulder
bladder	kidneys	spine
brain	liver	thigh
calf	lungs	throat
chest	mouth	toe
elbow	neck	torso
finger	palm	waist
forearm	pancreas	wrist

It REALLY Hurts...

aching	infected	scalded
achy	inflamed	septic
agonizing	irritated	sharp
blistered	itchy	smarting
bruised	nagging	sore
burning	painful	stinging
burnt	pounding	swollen
chafed	prickly	tender
festering	puffy	throbbing
hurting	raw	tingling

Sun, Sea, & Sand

harbor	seashells	beach chair
pier	seashore	beach towel
surf	seaweed	beach umbrella
tides	diving	Frisbee
waves	floating	Jet Ski
cliffs	paddling	sand bucket
coast	surfing	spade
pebbles	swimming	sunglasses
rock pool	beach ball	sunscreen
rocks	beach buggy	surfboard

HAPPY ENDINGS V

angelic	dynamic	magic
artistic	elastic	plastic
athletic	electric	poetic
atomic	energetic	public
basic	epic	robotic
classic	exotic	sonic
comic	frantic	static
cosmic	hectic	titanic
domestic	historic	toxic
dramatic	ironic	tragic

PARTY TIME!

balloon volleyball

blindman's buff

charades

cornhole

follow-the-leader

guessing games

hide-and-seek

horseshoes

hunt the slipper

I spy

karaoke

Limbo

mummy wrap

musical chairs

piñata

red light, green light

red rover

sack race

scavenger hunt

Simon Says

tag

three-legged race

treasure hunt

tug-of-war

water balloon toss

THAT'S A PROPER WORD?!

alakazam

bada bing

brouhaha

clodhopper

collywobbles

comeuppance

diddle

dillydally

dollop

gallivant

harum-scarum

hobnob

humbug

jabberwocky

piffle

ramshackle

scallywag

shenanigans

shilly-shally

skedaddle

squeegee

tootle

umpteen

vamoose

wishy-washy

INDEX

In the following entries, the letter 'A' refers to the upper list on the page, while 'B' refers to the lower one.

Made in United States
Troutdale, OR
12/18/2024